25 Days of Jesus

An Advent Journey through the Gospel of Luke

By Jennifer Bryant

ISBN # 978-1-7377468-1-2

TABLE OF CONTENTS

Dedicated to Grandma Iris Logan, who carried on favorite family traditions, and always made our Christmas time warm and special.
Thank you for letting me play with your typewriter. You are dearly loved and missed every day.

Forward

We were rushing through Walmart on a sunny December day in Southern California. Mom wanted to pick up some gift bags and stocking stuffers for the younger kids, and I was her tag-a-long assistant after school.

As Mom darted her cart through the crowds of hurried shoppers, I noticed my favorite colorful jars stacked like soldiers on the end aisle display.

"Mom! Can I get this candle? *Sniff... Mmmmmm,* it smells like a Christmas tree." She grinned and let me add it to our basket.

Seasonal candles were my favorite thing as a kid. They were a sign to me that a magical time was coming, and each smell prepared my spirit to get caught up in the fanciful festivities of Christmas. Even the name of each candle was whimsical: Snowy Fir, Gingerbread Cookie, Peppermint Stick.

I wanted the one that a freshly-snowed forest. Balsam, cedar, spruce. Smells are very important to me. Smells instantly transport me to past memories and into imaginary worlds. But we had to drive an hour up to the mountains for anything that resembled a forest.

I grew up in a busy city, next to a liquor store parking lot and a major intersection. The smells of tire rubber, gas, and exhaust were first to hit my senses. As the oldest of four kids, our household bustled with sounds and scents of family life, too. Diapers, dish water, damp towels, and dirty socks were in no short supply.

As soon as I was allowed to click a long-neck lighter, I was lighting candles. I loved how such a small light could fill an entire room, and create a warming mood. That small flame released a powerful fragrance that wrapped us in all the goodness of the holiday.

I wonder what it smelled like on that first Christmas night, in the manger of Bethlehem. If you've ever spent time around barn animals, you don't need to wonder. I'm sure it was not exactly peppermint sticks and cinnamon pinecones.

We get to experience the wonderful smells of celebration because God chose to come down to this dusty world as a baby. He lived among us, and eventually sacrificed Himself so we could experience to joy of His love and presence in our lives.

As you walk through this devotional with your family, we will begin with the Christmas story, and walk through each chapter of the Gospel of Luke. Instead of just the manger scene, we will look at the whole picture: the life and purpose of Jesus on earth.

In between devotions, sing each classic Christmas song together, and notice how the lyrics teach about God's love for His people. Treat it like a Bible study if you like, and look up the corresponding scriptures.

Christmas time may bring back memories for you. Sweet ones of baked goods, or cedar trees. But Christmas might also remind you of difficult times. Remember this: God knows every season of life we go through and He promises to be close to us. His Spirit stayed with us even after Jesus resurrected, and is with us even now. Do you believe that?

The blessing of Christmas is that Christ came to redeem us back to Himself. Redemption is about restoring what has once been broken, forgotten, or left worthless. His birth, life, and death is our great hope because we regain purpose as precious creations of a living God.

Decide in your heart what you will do with this Christmas season. The old times have passed away. Keep the good memories and carry them forward. Create a new season of new memories, and new traditions, but never forget the original reason why we celebrate.

Take in all the wondrous scents of Christmas, and hold each other close. Read and pray together for advent, not as another thing for the to-do list, but to solidify the bonds of your family relationship. Light your candles, bake delicious treats, and gather together in the memory, acceptance and grace of what Jesus did for you.

How to Use this Devotional

Advent Calendar

Follow along for the first 25 days of December and look up the corresponding Bible verses before reading that day's devotion. Some days have a classic Christmas carol after each reading.

Christmas Songs

Every song published here has lyrics based in scripture. Look up each scripture reference below the song and discuss the Biblical message with your family. Use our playlist here for easy access: https://practicalfamily.org/25DaysJesusSongs

Recipes

Choose any of our 12 recipes to try out for holiday parties or cozy family time at home. Download the entire recipe book here: http://practicalfamily.org/25DaysJesusRecipes

BONUS: Audio Book

Download the audio version of each devotional to play for your individual or family devotional time. Read by the author.
Purchase here:
https://practicalfamily.org/25DaysJesusAudioBook

Extra Resources

See the back of the book for more goodies available through Practical Family.

Advent Calendar

The Christmas season is finally here! This is what **advent** means: the arrival of a much-awaited time. Follow these December days as a pathway instead of a calendar & re-use this devotional every year as you await the celebration of the birth of our Savior.

Dec 1 Luke 1:32-33	**Dec 2** Luke 2:9-11 *Angels We Have Heard on High*	**Dec 3** Luke 3:21-22	**Dec 4** Luke 4:1-2 *Away in a Manger*	**Dec 5** Luke 5:10-11
Dec 6 Luke 6:27-28 *Do You Hear What I Hear?*	**Dec 7** Luke 7:22-23	**Dec 8** Luke 8:15 *Hark the Herald Angels Sing*	**Dec 9** Luke 9:20-22	**Dec 10** Luke 10:41-42 *Joy to the World*
Dec 11 Luke 11:9-10	**Dec 12** Luke 12:22-23;24 *What Child Is This?*	**Dec 13** Luke 13:12-13	**Dec 14** Luke 14:11 *O Come, All Ye Faithful*	**Dec 15** Luke 15:10
Dec 16 Luke 16:13 *O Come, O Come Emmanuel*	**Dec 17** Luke 17:20-21	**Dec 18** Luke 18:16-17 *O Holy Night*	**Dec 19** Luke 19:36-38	**Dec 20** Luke 20:17 *O Little Town of Bethlehem*
Dec 21 Luke 21:5-6	**Dec 22** Luke 22:19-20; 41-42 *Silent Night*	**Dec 23** Luke 23:46-47	**Dec 24** Luke 24:44-47 *The First Noel*	**Dec 25** Luke 24:48-49

December 1

He will be great and will be called the Son of the Most High; and the Lord God will give Him the throne of His father David; and He will reign over the house of Jacob forever, and His kingdom will have no end. Luke 1:32-33

Devotional

The God of heaven saw fit to send the most important message to a young girl from a small town. Mary had a most important assignment. She would serve as a vessel to deliver the Son of the Most High safely into this world. It was an incredible fulfillment of prophecy through the blood lines of King David, all the way back to Jacob.

God had a plan to save His people from the moment sin entered the Garden (Genesis 3), but it was not a quick fix. It was a process, drawn out over centuries, with many chances for a rebellious and self-serving people to turn back to their Creator and trust Him with their lives. God continued to be good, just, and most of all, patient. He sees every one of us, and wants to speak to our heart about His plan for our lives.

Just as Mary's assignment came at a specific time in history, God is unfolding events in our world according to His perfect plan. You might be in a waiting pattern today. Waiting for the Christmas season to arrive so the traditions and feel-good activities might bring your family closer together. Maybe you're waiting for a child to come around and show a spark of interest in all your effort to love them. Maybe this is your first Christmas without a loved one, and you need more time to heal and grieve. Just remember, God is faithful.

As He waits for us, He prepares a way back, provides comfort and rest in our brokenness, and an open door to run into His arms as our loving Father. He is faithful from beginning to end.

Prayer

Lord, help me to trust the plan You've had for my life from the very beginning. Thank You for the gift of time and second chances to come back to You in honesty and sincerity. Help my unbelief when the days are difficult. Amen.

December 2

And an angel of the Lord suddenly stood before them, and the glory of the Lord shone around them; and they were terribly frightened. But the angel said to them, "Do not be afraid; for behold, I bring you good news of great joy which will be for all the people; for today in the city of David there has been born for you a Savior, who is Christ the Lord. Luke 2:9-11

Devotional

It's the classic picture of the angels appearing to poor shepherds in the field, and another example of the humble beginnings of our Savior. It wasn't a dazzling presentation in the courts of kings and high priests. No—it was a dazzling presentation in the night sky for the lowliest of men. Not for a large crowd, but for a chosen few.

But why shepherds? My guess is that these individuals knew what it was like to care for sheep who would wander from the fold, fall into ditches, or follow the crowd over a cliff. Jesus himself would eventually compare us to sheep, but also to declare His love for even one who wandered away. The angels gave a sign: a baby, wrapped in swaddling clothes, lying in a feeding trough. It was a simple message without elaborate explanation, but when they followed, they found great hope.

As parents, we know the tendencies of our kids, whether we've got quiet and timid or rough and rowdy little people at home. Just like these shepherds, we become afraid when we don't quite know what God is doing.

But as Jesus came to be our shepherd, He helps us to lead and care for our precious ones as well. When you allow Him to lead you, you will hear His voice to find the hope you need.

Prayer

Lord, thank You for leading and guiding me with my kids. I don't know where You're leading them, but I trust that Your plan is good. Help me to find joy in everyday circumstances and believe that You are faithfully leading me to good places. Amen.

Angels We Have Heard on High

Angels we have heard on high
Sweetly singing o'er the plains
And the mountains in reply
Echoing their joyous strains

Gloria, in excelsis Deo!
Gloria, in excelsis Deo!

Shepherds, why this jubilee?
Why your joyous strains prolong?
What the gladsome tidings be
Which inspire your heavenly song?

Come to Bethlehem and see
Him Whose birth the angels sing;
Come, adore on bended knee,
Christ the Lord, the newborn King.

See Him in a manger laid
Jesus, Lord of heaven and earth;
Mary, Joseph, lend your aid,
With us sing our Savior's birth.

Isaiah 9:6

Matthew 2

Luke 2:10-13

Revelation 19:16

Edward Shippen Barnes & James Chadwick, Traditional French Carol, Public Domain

Hot Apple Cider

- 4 cups apple cider (bottled or from packets)
- 1 apple (sliced)
- 1 orange (sliced)
- 3 cinnamon sticks
- 2 slices fresh ginger (about 1" each, or 1/4 tsp ground ginger)
- 1 teaspoon whole allspice (or 1/2 tsp ground allspice or 1/2 tsp pumpkin pie spice

Stove Top
Add all ingredients to a medium sized pot. Bring to a simmer (low heat), and continue to simmer for 15-20 minutes. Serve hot and garnish with slice of apple, orange, or cinnamon stick.

Crockpot
Add all ingredients to the crock pot and set on low for 3-4 hours.

Strain out fruit before refrigerating.
Reheat and serve hot.

December 3

Now when all the people were baptized, Jesus was also baptized, and while He was praying, heaven was opened, and the Holy Spirit descended upon Him in bodily form like a dove, and a voice came out of heaven, "You are My beloved Son, in You I am well-pleased. Luke 3:21-22

Devotional

In less than one chapter, that baby in the manger had grown into a man. The beginning of His ministry was marked with a handoff from John the Baptist (Jesus' earthly cousin) as the one who would prepare His way. We see the Holy Spirit in the form of a dove, which in Jewish tradition, would have been the lesser animal to bring for temple sacrifice. Another example of humble beginnings.

The declaration is one to consider: a voice from heaven, an affirmation of God's pleasure on this man from Nazareth — not the son of Joseph, but from a higher source. The declaration was made in the midst of others being baptized, so it was evident that the life of this man would be set apart from the rest.

Do you believe that God has set you apart for a purpose? Through Jesus, we are now able to be sons and daughters of the Most High God. His life, death, and resurrection made it possible to confidently join the family of God. Just as the Father blessed the earthly ministry of Jesus, we can be bold to proclaim His goodness in our lives.

Prayer

Lord, thank You for loving us as sons and daughters. Let Jesus' ministry on earth prove again and again in my life that Your love and protection wraps me in love and light. May I never forget that You're with me on that journey. Amen.

December 4

Jesus, full of the Holy Spirit, returned from the Jordan and was led around by the Spirit in the wilderness for forty days, being tempted by the devil. And He ate nothing during those days, and when they had ended, He became hungry. Luke 4:1-2

Devotional

From Jesus' baptism to the dry and lonely desert wilderness, He carried the Spirit with Him into this experience. This was a necessary experience for Him, and while we may not understand every reason, one thing is for certain: we can trust that He was faced with temptation in the same ways we struggle every day.

The God of the Universe faced the effects of sin when He entered our world, and while living in a human body did not make Jesus a sinful being, the choice to sin was still present. He modeled to us a life lived righteously even in the face of hunger, oppression, and disloyalty. Through the power of the Spirit of God, He resisted, and so can we.

It is difficult to grasp, but our wilderness experiences are necessary for growth. We need to experience a complete reliance on God in order to face difficulties with humility and grace. We need to endure and persevere to build physical, mental, and spiritual resilience. How amazing is it that we have a God who can understand our weakness? He is not only aware, but walking right beside us.

Prayer

Thank You for meeting me right where I am, and for living a human life to show me how close You have been to my struggle. Help me to learn from the difficult times and lead my kids through their own trials. Help me to rely on Your Spirit when I feel like I can't go any further. Amen.

Away In a Manger

Away in a manger, no crib for a bed,
The little Lord Jesus
Laid down his sweet head.
The stars in the sky
Looked down where he lay,
The little Lord Jesus
Asleep in the hay.

The cattle are lowing, the baby awakes,
But little Lord Jesus
No crying he makes.
I love Thee, Lord Jesus,
Look down from the sky
And stay by my cradle
Til morning is nigh.

Be near me, Lord Jesus,
I ask Thee to stay
Close by me forever
And love me, I pray.
Bless all the dear children
In thy tender care,
And take us to heaven,
To live with Thee there.

Luke 2:10-13

John 14

James Ramsey Murray, John Thomas McFarland, & Martin Luther, late 1800s. Public Domain.

Spinach & Bacon Quiche
with Sweet Potato Crust

- 2 Sweet Potatoes (medium, orange color, peeled, sliced 1/8" or 4 cups shredded)
- 3 slices bacon, diced
- 2 garlic cloves
- 1 yellow onion, diced
- 8 large eggs
- 3/4 cup milk (can use almond milk)
- 1/8 tsp ground nutmeg
- 1 handful grated cheese (cheddar or jack)
- 16 oz. chopped spinach (frozen bag thawed or 2 cups fresh)
- 4 Tbsp coconut oil (separate 2 Tbsp each)

1. Preheat oven to 360°
2. Grease bottom and sides of round quiche dish with coconut oil
3. Peel and slice sweet potatoes and arrange circles on dish to cover bottom & sides.
4. Bake at 360° for 15 minutes.
5. While crust is baking, warm 2 Tbsp coconut oil in frying pan.
6. Sauteé garlic & onion until fragrant.
7. Stir often to prevent burning. Add spinach & cook down until crust is ready.
8. Remove cooked mixture, add diced bacon & cook until sizzling. Add to spinach mixture & spread over sweet potato crust.
9. Scramble eggs with milk, cheese, & nutmeg. Pour into crust.
10. Bake for 25-30 minutes. Serves 6-8.

December 5

And Jesus said to Simon, "Do not fear, from now on you will be catching men." When they had brought their boats to land, they left everything and followed Him. Luke 5:10b-11

Devotional

After a full night of work with nothing to show for it, this carpenter-turned-Rabbi shows up and tells a bunch of fishermen how to do their job. With nothing left to lose, they throw their nets out into deep water, only to be surprised with two boats full of catch.

This passage reveals a couple of amazing things. First, provision for the fishermen when there was no hope after their effort, and second, enough trust in the words of a simple teacher to leave that livelihood and follow Him. Have you experienced the power of God in your life? Enough to give up the most important things in your life to follow Him? The question is less about stuff than it is about your faith in a God who can do immeasurably more than you can ask or think.

God equips us after we're willing to follow Him. All we need to do is believe He is able. Think of the most difficult, impossible things you have to handle right now. Do you believe He can turn things around? Do you trust Him in the deep water? Let Him navigate your life today.

Prayer

Lord, I admit that I've been trying to do a lot in my own strength. It's frustrating to work so hard and see so little return. Help me to trust You and to remember to give everything into Your hands, and to believe You want to do so much more with my obedience than I can do on my own. Amen.

December 6

But I say to you who hear, love your enemies, do good to those who hate you, bless those who curse you, pray for those who mistreat you. Luke 6:27-28

Devotional

This is one teaching that made first-century folks scratch their heads. Be kind to my enemies? To the people who enslaved my people for hundreds of years? The same people who have taken away our human rights and basic freedoms?

Kindness in the face of evil is not a natural human response, but it can be divinely inspired by the Holy Spirit. Jesus was speaking to His disciples in this passage. Luke says He turned His gaze toward them, specifically. They would be responsible for spreading the gospel, and this teaching was the foundation of their training!

Parents, we have that same responsibility: to be ambassadors of the gospel in our home first, and then the world. Think about how you naturally react to difficult people and situations. This is not about becoming a doormat or allowing yourself to be taken advantage of, but do you try to practice more gracious responses? Your family will notice.

Our kids will emulate the attitudes we display within the walls of our home, driving on the roads, and in mixed company. Do your best to model kindness, beginning with difficult people who may cross your path this holiday season. Ask God for an extra dose of grace and agape love.

Prayer

Lord, I need Your help to agape love others. Please open my eyes to the people in my life who need that kind of unconditional love. Teach me how not to be easily offended and when to take that extra step to pray for those who have mistreated me. I want to witness Your goodness when these feelings don't come as naturally to me. Amen.

Do You Hear What I Hear?

Said the night wind to the
little lamb
Do you see what I see?
Way up in the sky little lamb
Do you see what I see?

A star, a star
Dancing in the night
With a tail as big as a kite
With a tail as big as a kite

Said the little lamb to the
shepherd boy
Do you hear what I hear?
Ringing through the sky
shepherd boy
Do you hear what I hear?

A song, a song
High above the tree
With a voice as big as the
sea
With a voice as big as the
sea

Said the shepherd boy to the
mighty king
Do you know what I know?
In your palace wall mighty king
Do you know what I know?

A child, a child
Shivers in the cold
Let us bring him silver and gold
Let us bring him silver and gold

Said the king to the people
everywhere
Listen to what I say
Pray for peace people
everywhere
Listen to what I say

The child, the child
Sleeping in the night
He will bring us goodness and
light!
He will bring us goodness and
light!

Luke 2:10-13

John 1:14;12:46

Make Ahead
French Toast Casserole

- 1 package brioche bread
- 8 eggs, large
- 2 cups milk
- 1/4 cup maple syrup
- 1 Tbsp vanilla extract
- 1/2 tsp salt
- 1 tsp cinnamon
- 1/4 tsp nutmeg
- 2 Tbsp coconut oil
- 1 cup pecans, chopped (optional)

Topping
- 1/2 cup light brown sugar
- 1 tsp cinnamon
- 4 Tbsp salted butter, sliced cold

Prepare and Chill Overnight
1. Grease 9'x13' baking dish with coconut oil
2. Cut bread into 1' cubes and layer in dish with chopped pecans
3. Whisk together eggs, milk, syrup, vanilla, salt, cinnamon, & nutmeg
4. Pour over bread & pecans
5. Cover with foil and chill for 4-6 hours

Ready to Bake
1. Remove casserole from refrigerator & preheat oven to 350°
2. Mix brown sugar, cinnamon, & sliced butter together. Crumble over casserole
3. Cover dish with foil & bake at 350° for 30 minutes.
4. Uncover & bake for another 20 minutes.
5. Let cool, then slice & serve with powdered sugar & maple syrup. Serves 8-10.

December 7

And He answered and said to them, "Go and report to John what you have seen and heard: the blind receive sight, the lame walk, the lepers are cleansed, and the deaf hear, the dead are raised up, the poor have the gospel preached to them. Blessed is he who does not take offense at Me. Luke 7:22-23

Devotional

The disciples of John are sent on a mission: to find out once and for all if Jesus is the One they have waited for. But Jesus does not give them a straight answer. Instead, He reminds them of the circumstances they have witnessed: the blind, lame, lepers, deaf, the poor and the dead are being healed left and right! These humanly impossible feats are being accomplished in their presence, all facts that cannot be denied.

When you read through the Gospels, you will find that Jesus would not often give direct answers when the answer could be derived from one's personal witness. He pointed people to the power of their own testimony. This would be the avenue by which the gospel of salvation would be spread to the entire world.

Have you witnessed circumstances in your life that can only be explained by the supernatural power of God? Maybe you came to know God after a miraculous turn of events, or the fulfillment of a whispered promise that pointed you back to His goodness. These gifts are special reminders from our Creator that He loves you and wants you to know His unchanging character.

Live as a witness of His love this season. Nobody can argue with the results of a changed life.

Prayer

Lord, thank You for your miraculous work in my life! Forgive me when I forget to be thankful for the milestones of how good You have been to me. Help me to take advantage of teachable moments with my kids, not just to pass on information, but to share the stories of how You've changed me for the better. Amen.

December 8

But the seed in the good soil, these are the ones who have heard the word in an honest and good heart, and hold it fast, and bear fruit with perseverance. Luke 8:15

Devotional

The Parable of the Sower was told in two parts in Luke's Gospel: the first part was for the crowd, where Jesus shared this metaphorical story and effectively allowed the seed of His words to scatter among the crowd. Each person was given the opportunity to interpret the meaning for their own life.

But to His disciples, Jesus elaborated and attached His meaning to each metaphor: the seed is the word of God, there are some from whom the devil steals God's truth, some have shallow roots and cannot absorb it, and some are immature and distracted by the pleasures of life. Those who will hear and receive, are teachable and will bear the good fruit of the Spirit (Galatians 5:22).

If you are reading this devotional, you are already preparing your heart to receive and learn from God's word. You are also being prepared as a Sower. Just as the Father granted the disciples a level of spiritual discernment, we can see this same lesson as an encouragement when we share the gospel.

It is ultimately not up to us how someone receives the truth and conviction of the Lord, but we are still called to scatter seed. We have the chance to scatter and also explain God's truth to our kids so that He can begin to work on their hearts through His Spirit. We can walk them through meaningful holiday traditions that point back to Jesus and remind them He is the reason we celebrate. Then step back, and let God do the rest.

Prayer

Lord, thank You for trusting me with the knowledge and discernment of Your beautiful word. Please help me to see where I end and You begin, and to know when to speak and when to trust that You're at work. Please show me how to help prepare the soil of my kids' hearts and how to answer their questions as they grow. Amen.

Hark the Herald Angels

Hark! the herald angels sing,
"Glory to the newborn King!"
Peace on earth, and mercy mild,
God and sinners reconciled
Joyful, all ye nations, rise,
Join the triumph of the skies;
With th' angelic host proclaim,
"Christ is born in Bethlehem."
Hark! the herald angels sing,
"Glory to the newborn King!"

Christ, by highest heav'n adored:
Christ, the everlasting Lord;
Late in time behold him come,
Offspring of the favored one.
Veil'd in flesh, the Godhead see;
Hail, th'incarnate Deity:
Pleased, as man, with men to dwell,
Jesus, our Emmanuel!
Hark! the herald angels sing,
"Glory to the newborn King!"

Hail! the heav'n born Prince of peace!
Hail! the Son of Righteousness!
Light and life to all He brings,
Risen with healing in his wings
Mild he lays his glory by,
Born that man no more may die:
Born to raise the sons of earth,
Born to give them second birth.
Hark! the herald angels sing,
"Glory to the newborn King!"

Isaiah 7:14   Luke 2:10-13   Philippians 2:5-11

Matthew 1:23   John 3

Charles Wesley, & Felix Mendelssohn-Bartholdy, 1739, Public Domain

Turkey Cranberry Pinwheels

- 4 green spinach tortillas
- 8 oz cream cheese, softened
- 1/2 cup dried cranberries
- 12 oz turkey slices
- 8 oz Havarti cheese slices
- Romaine lettuce leaves, without ribs

1. Mix together cream cheese, & cranberries
2. Place two tortillas side by side, overlap slightly
3. Spread mixture over both tortillas
4. Layer turkey, cheese, & lettuce
5. Turn tortilla sides inward and roll tightly like a burrito.
6. For easier cutting, wrap in plastic wrap & store in refrigerator for an hour.
7. Ready to serve: slice into 1' pieces. Leftovers can store for 2 days. Serves 2-4.

December 9

And He said to them, "But who do you say that I am?" And Peter answered and said, "The Christ of God." But He warned them and instructed them not to tell this to anyone, saying, "The Son of Man must suffer many things and be rejected by the elders and chief priests and scribes, and be killed and be raised up on the third day. Luke 9:20-22

Devotional

This question is probably one of the most profound in all of the New Testament: Who do you say that I am? Some translations say, "The Christ, Son of the Living God." Jesus asked his disciples, the closest people to Him, and still asked them not to share this testimony. He would still have to suffer, die, and be resurrected for this title to hold power with those outside of His intimate circle.

Jesus fulfilled His purpose when He died for your sin and mine and then resurrected from the dead (appearing to hundreds of witnesses) to prove His divinity. He only asked his closest people to testify (remember the power of the testimony?) to what they had seen and heard based on their experiences with Him.

When you hang out with someone long enough, you become more acquainted with their patterns, responses, and consistency of character. Peter saw something much more than human, and his mouth testified of God.

Who do you say Jesus is? A good teacher, a prominent historical figure? A trusted friend? What you do with Jesus will determine how you see yourself.

If your relationship with Him is limited to good moral teaching, you might miss the transformative power of His divine nature. Dive deeper in your time with Jesus this week and watch how He can change you from the inside out.

Prayer

Lord, I want to know You better than I think I do. Help me as I read and pray to be open to Your leading and to witness the life of Jesus not as something in the past, but a testimony that is living and active and present in my life today. Amen.

December 10

But the Lord answered and said to her, "Martha, Martha, you are worried and bothered about so many things; but only one thing is necessary, for Mary has chosen the good part, which shall not be taken away from her. Luke 10:41-42

Devotional

Martha and Mary: two sisters who were close to Jesus during His ministry and among the few women specifically mentioned in scripture. Their special relationship with Him is highlighted and has been used to illustrate a place where we may find ourselves when the busyness of life catches up with us.

If you're a mom reading this, you may be familiar with the state of Martha's hurried request as opposed to Mary's calm demeanor at Jesus' feet. You may have even been encouraged to "be more like Mary," as the clear example of a woman to emulate.

But I'd like to challenge you with a different perspective. What if we notice instead the choices they were faced with at this moment in time? A meal needed to be prepared and someone had to do it. Martha chose to become flustered and asked Jesus (in an almost accusatory tone) if He cared that Mary was not contributing (because she certainly did). He called her by name (twice), and pointed out that her focus was scattered... and now she's worried about her sister, too?

If Martha's blunder was to make other's choices her responsibility, then I can totally relate.

We have lots of worries on our plate, don't we? We cannot possibly solve every problem or put out every fire. But we try. We try to save our kids from making mistakes, or apologize for things out of our control. We are worried about many things at the same time. But Jesus said, "one thing is necessary," (not many). Respect your sister's choice, because this one will last forever.

Prayer

Lord, help me to stop taking responsibility for the choices of others. Please help me to respect the choices of others and not take on more than I need to. Help me to rest in the comfort of knowing that You're right there with me and I only need to focus on one important thing at a time. Thank You for the gift of Your presence. Amen.

Joy to the World

Joy to the world, the Lord is come;
Let earth receive her King;
Let every heart prepare Him room,
And heaven and nature sing,
And heaven and nature sing,
And heaven, and heaven, and nature sing.

Joy to the earth, the Savior reigns;
Let men their songs employ;
While fields and floods,
Rocks, hills and plains
Repeat the sounding joy,
Repeat the sounding joy,
Repeat, repeat the sounding joy.

No more let sins and sorrows grow,
Nor thorns infest the ground;
He comes to make His blessings flow
Far as the curse is found,
Far as the curse is found,
Far as, far as the curse is found.

He rules the world with truth and grace,
And makes the nations prove
The glories of His righteousness,
And wonders of His love,
And wonders of His love,
And wonders, wonders of His love.

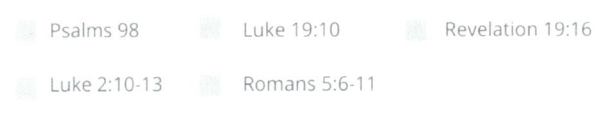

Psalms 98   Luke 19:10   Revelation 19:16

Luke 2:10-13   Romans 5:6-11

Gingerbread Oatmeal

- 1 cup rolled oats (gluten free)
- 1 1/2 cups water
- 1 cup milk (can use almond milk)
- 1/2 tsp cinnamon
- 1/4 tsp ginger
- 1/8 tsp cloves
- 1/8 tsp nutmeg
- 1/8 tsp allspice
- 1 Tsbp cashew or almond butter
- 1/2 tsp vanilla extract
- 2-3 Tbsp maple syrup or chopped apples (sweetener)
- Pinch of salt

1. Combine oats and water in medium sauce pan over medium heat. Bring to a low boil until oats begin to thicken. Turn off heat, keep pan on burner.
2. Add milk of your choice, spices, nut butter of your choice, vanilla, salt, and sweetener of your choice.
3. Thicker consistency: cook longer. If you prefer it runny, add more milk.
4. Garnish with cinnamon or Pumpkin Spice if desired.

Microwave Instructions: combine oats and water and heat for 2 minutes on high). Stir in remaining ingredients. Cover to keep warm until serving.

December 11

So I say to you, ask, and it will be given to you; seek, and you will find; knock, and it will be opened to you. For everyone who asks, receives; and he who seeks, finds; and to him who knocks, it will be opened. Luke 11:9-10

Devotional

Jesus' demonstration of prayer can be found in Matthew 6 and here at the beginning of Luke 11, and it was a direct response to his disciples' request to teach them. No doubt, they noticed His prayer life and relationship with the Father was special — not to mention Jesus' apparent favor in the performing of miracles.

"Teach us to pray..." and so He modeled the elements of prayer and a simple approach to God. But then He teaches them to keep asking. Yes, talk to God, but ask for the good gifts He wants to give you!

The Christmas season is a time of gift-giving and receiving, but how often are we asking God for more of Him? We can never ask God too many times. Continuing to come to Him is a good thing because it proves we know He's there.

There's also something about a continued request that reinforces how important that request is to us. Like when you listen to your child's request for something you hope they forget about soon. If they continue to ask over a longer period of time, it must be important, right?

Jesus impresses on his disciples that God is good, like a ather who wants to give His kids good things.

He's not holding out on us, He just knows what's better. But the door is always open to ask. Keep asking, seeking, knocking, and trust that He hears you.

Prayer

Lord, thank You for always being available. Teach me how to pray in a way that increases my faith that You are good no matter what. Thank You for coming and living a life that demonstrates how much you love me. Amen.

December 12

And He said to His disciples, "For this reason I say to you, do not worry about your life, as to what you will eat; nor for your body, as to what you will put on. For life is more than food, and the body more than clothing. Consider the ravens, for they neither sow nor reap; they have no storeroom nor barn, and yet God feeds them; how much more valuable you are than the birds!...For where your treasure is, there your heart will be also." Luke 12:22-24; 34

Devotional

Just as God is a good Father who loves to give us good gifts, He is also a Father who provides. This message was another from Jesus to His disciples, reminding them that God knows and cares for them. In fact, He shares several parables that demonstrate the heart of those who care more about money and possessions than a right relationship with God.

Our value is much more than what we own. If we think that our value lies only in what we can earn, and these things are able to be destroyed, then we are not seeing ourselves as valuable as God sees us.

It's tempting, during the Christmas season, to purchase many things to prove our own or someone else's value. It's tempting to measure our own worth in how many presents are under the tree with our name on it. But if you never received one more earthly present in your life, would that change how you see yourself? Because God would still call you precious.

We will worship the things that we think about most, whether it's clothing, jewelry, houses, or even food. God wants our whole heart to be satisfied with Him and trust that His provision is enough. Live like you're enough today and love Him more than stuff.

Prayer

Lord, thank You for always providing for my every need! You are good and You have blessed me with more than enough. Help me to practice gratitude every day. Amen.

What Child Is This?

What Child is this who, laid to rest
On Mary's lap is sleeping?
Whom Angels greet with anthems sweet,
While shepherds watch are keeping?

This, this is Christ the King,
Whom shepherds guard and Angels sing;
Haste, haste, to bring Him laud,
The Babe, the Son of Mary.

Why lies He in such mean estate,
Where ox and lamb are feeding?
Good Christians, fear, for sinners here
The silent Word is pleading.

Nails, spear shall pierce Him through,
The cross be borne for me, for you.
Hail, hail the Word made flesh,
The Babe, the Son of Mary.

So bring Him incense, gold and myrrh,
Come peasant, king to own Him;
The King of kings salvation brings,
Let loving hearts enthrone Him.

Raise, raise a song on high,
The Virgin sings her lullaby.
Joy, joy for Christ is born,
The Babe, the Son of Mary.

Isaiah 7:14	Luke 2	1 Timothy 6:15
Matthew 27	Luke 23	Revelation 17:14, 19:11–16

William Chatterton Dix, 1865. Adapted from Dix's poem *The Manger Throne*. Music: "Greensleeves," 16th Century English melody. Arranged by Sir John Stainer.

Cranberry Pecan Cheese Ball

- 8 ounces cream cheese (soften at room temp)
- 1 cup white sharp cheddar (shredded)
- 1 cup dried cranberries (chopped and divided)
- 1 cup pecans chopped (toast if desired)
- 1/4 cup chives or green onions chopped
- 1/2 tsp garlic powder
- 1/8 tsp cinnamon
- 1/8 tsp nutmeg

1. **Toasted Pecans:** Pre-heat oven to 375°. Chop pecans with a thick knife, and place on baking tray or cookie sheet. Bake for 5 minutes or until aromatic. Remove from oven and set aside.
2. In a large bowl, beat cream cheese, cheddar cheese, 1/2 cup toasted pecans, 1/2 cup cranberries, chives or green onions, garlic powder, cinnamon, and nutmeg until well combined.
3. Lay out a foot of plastic wrap or parchment paper. Place cheese mixture in the center and cover completely with wrap to form into a ball. Place in fridge until ready to serve.
4. Just before serving, combine remaining 1/2 cup pecans, 1/2 dried cranberries, and 2 Tbsp chives on a flat surface or cutting board. Unwrap the ball and roll in cranberry-pecan mixture.
5. Serve with pita chips, gluten-free crackers, pretzels, carrots, celery, or apples.

Appetizer version - Chop nuts smaller and roll cheese mixture smaller (size of golf balls) and place a pretzel stick in the center (easy to pick up from a platter). Tie with a decorative string at the base of pretzel stick.

December 13

When Jesus saw her, He called her over and said to her, "Woman, you are freed from your sickness." And He laid His hands on her; and immediately she was made erect again and began glorifying God. Luke 13:12-13

Devotional

I believe Jesus was in the business of setting people free. I wish I could have been there to see the gleam in His eyes when broken and hurting people were made whole. This particular woman was plagued by a spirit that caused her to walk around bent over. Can you imagine? Living for eighteen years upside down? Jesus came to turn her life right-side up and to free her from the bondage of a disoriented life.

Maybe that's the Jesus you need to meet this year. You may be used to celebrating the baby in the manger, but the point of this entire devotional experience is to show you that baby's real life and purpose on this earth and in our lives today.

What needs to be made right-side up in your life today? Is there something about this season that is particularly rough for you? God wants to set us free from the bondage of harsh words, bad memories, and the pain of this life that should not plague us any longer than necessary.

As with the healed woman in this passage, the evidence of a changed life looks more like praise than pessimism. Ask God to set you free today. He wants you to ask! Keep on coming to Him, because He wants to give you good things.

Prayer

Lord, I need to believe that You can make anything right, even when I think it's impossible. You heal so many, and I know You can heal my broken parts too, on the inside and out. Thank You for the freedom that comes from knowing You. Amen.

December 14

For everyone who exalts himself will be humbled, and he who humbles himself will be exalted. Luke 14:11

Devotional

Jesus spent most of His time with the disciples; men who loved, trusted, and wanted to learn from Him. But as His popularity grew, He would also be invited to the homes of wealthy men and be in the company of the religious leaders who wanted to catch him in a blasphemous statement. These men were also threatened by the increasing influence Jesus had over the people.

To the Pharisees and other church leaders, prominence, affluence, and influence were the highest and most authoritative trust factors of the day. Many became power hungry and Jesus didn't hesitate to call them on their hypocrisy. Their attitudes were in direct opposition to the gospel and everything the Holy Scriptures revealed God to be.

If we're not checking our hearts with the Lord often, our human spirit can be lured away by things like power and influence, or the positive attention that money can bring. But these things are not what really exalt us, Jesus says. It's the humility of our heart that God sees, and that kind of lowliness of spirit will attract friends who love you as you are, not for what you have.

We cannot operate out of a heart of entitlement or believe that a certain level of comfort is deserved. We cannot ride through life on the faith of our parents or loved ones.

Our relationship with Christ must be our own: tested and tried and made pure by God. Ask Him to search your heart today and show you areas where entitlement may have crept in. Ask Him to keep you humble by considering others first.

Prayer

Lord, forgive me if I've been operating as if I deserve more than I do. Help me to be honest with myself and my attitude toward You and others. Help me to live in a way that serves others before myself. Amen.

O Come, All Ye Faithful

O come, all ye faithful,
Joyful and triumphant,
O come ye, O come ye to Bethlehem;
Come and behold him,
Born the King of angels;

O come, let us adore him,
O come, let us adore him,
O Come, let us adore him, Christ the Lord

Sing, choirs of angels,
Sing in exultation,
Sing, all ye citizens of heaven above;
Glory to God
In the highest...

O come, let us adore him,
O come, let us adore him,
O Come, let us adore him, Christ the Lord

Yea, Lord, we greet thee,
Born this happy morning;
Jesus, to thee be glory given;
Word of the Father,
Now in flesh appearing...

O come, let us adore him,
O come, let us adore him,
O Come, let us adore him, Christ the Lord

Luke 2:7-20

John 1

Hebrews 1:4

Chicken Strawberry Salad
with Champagne Vinaigrette

This beautifully colorful salad pops with Christmas festivity and serves as a healthy side dish or main meal

- 8 oz bag spinach leaves (wash and spin)
- 6 oz roasted or rotisserie chicken (shredded)
- 6 oz fresh strawberries (sliced)
- Handful of candied pecans (or favorite nut mix)
- Girard's Champagne Vinaigrette
- Diced avocado (optional or to replace chicken for veggie option)

Combine all ingredients and toss before serving.

December 15

In the same way, I tell you, there is joy in the presence of the angels of God over one sinner who repents. Luke 15:10

Devotional

Jesus gives us a glimpse of heaven here. The angels rejoice when a lost soul finds their way back to God. We can trust the red letters of Jesus, especially if your answer to the question, "Who do you say that I am ?" is "God incarnate." He was there!

As Jesus continues to show us through His life and ministry, He explained through many parables and examples that the heart of God is to rescue, support, and love those who wander. Those who believe they are self-sufficient and have life figured out are less likely to see all that God has in store. That's the difference. Hearts who are dependent on God are much more likely to see His work in their lives than hearts dependent on self.

You've probably had a glimpse into this. Some of the most frustrating years as parents are the "all by myself" years. Of course we want them to learn from their mistakes and be independent, but that same stubborn tenacity can be applied to relationships in later years. God gives us freedom within safe boundaries, and always an open door to return when we wander too far.

Maybe you have a wanderer in the family this Christmas. Maybe it's your own heart that has felt far from God. It's never too late to turn back. Rest in knowing that there is no condemnation upon return, just wide open arms of a Father who never left.

Prayer

Lord, I know I can be stubborn at times when life doesn't seem to be going according to plan. Help to soften my heart toward Your perfect will today, and to open myself to those who are making their own choices. Help me to have that same joy and respond with love and grace when others turn back to You. Amen.

December 16

No servant can serve two masters; for either he will hate the one and love the other, or else he will be devoted to one and despise the other. You cannot serve God and wealth. Luke 16:13

Devotional

Jesus was clear about His ministry on earth, and in His limited amount of time, chose to journey from town to town and teach as many who would listen. This kind of lifestyle may have seemed "unstable" to those who needed to support a family, but He lived a life fully dependent on the Father.

This middle part of Luke seemed fully dedicated to warning against the love of money and power, as the Pharisees represented a type of spiritual oppression on the common and uneducated people. Jesus attempted to ease their minds by showing them that a dedication to money without trust in God is like serving two separate entities. Money is not evil, per se, but a heart that chases wealth as a means to an end can block a real and honest relationship with God.

The holiday season can certainly test our loyalties in this area. We want to provide a million magical moments for our kids, and oftentimes this comes at the expense of emptying our bank accounts. When the gifts don't feel like enough, or not as much as another family, we begin to panic and throw every ounce of energy into earning more, or taking on more debt to fit an unrealistic mold of what Christmas should be.

Have you placed the need for more money in front of God's ability to provide for you without it? Have your commitments to work or side job taken the place of your time with family or the Lord? Take some time to re-prioritize and ask yourself, "If this all went away tomorrow, would I still be satisfied with Jesus?

Prayer

Lord, please help me never to lose sight of that special and personal connection You've offered to me. Help me to see if I've been fearful of not having money and placed that in front of trusting You with all things. Remind me of the things we truly need and the things that are extra. Help my soul to be satisfied with You. Amen.

O Come, O Come Emmanuel

O come, O come, Emmanuel,
And ransom captive Israel,
That mourns in lonely exile here
Until the Son of God appears.

Rejoice! Rejoice! Emmanuel
Shall come to thee, O Israel.

O come, Thou Rod of Jesse, free
Thine own from Satan's tyranny;
From depths of hell Thy people save,
And give them victory o'er the grave.

O come, Thou Day-Spring, come and cheer
Our spirits by Thine advent here;
Disperse the gloomy clouds of night
And death's dark shadows put to flight!

O come, Thou Key of David, come,
And open wide our heavenly home;
Make safe the way that leads on high,
And close the path to misery.

O come, O come, Thou Lord of Might,
Who to Thy tribes on Sinai's height
In ancient times didst give the law
In cloud, and majesty, and awe.

Exodus 19   1 Corinthians 15:54-58

Isaiah 11:1; 22:22   Revelation 3:7

Matthew 1:23

Christmas Crepes
Sweet or Savory

Great for breakfast, lunch, dinner, or dessert!

- 1 1/2 c. Flour
- 1 Tbsp. Sugar
- 1/2 tsp. Salt
- 1/2 tsp. Baking Powder
- 2 c. Milk
- 1/2 tsp. Vanilla
- 2 Large Eggs
- 2 Tbsp. Melted Butter (to coat the pan)

1. Mix dry ingredients, then add to wet ingredients. Whisk until smooth.
2. Heat large frying pan to medium & brush with butter before every crepe.
3. Drop a ladle full (or 1/4 cup) of batter into the pan and turn pan to coat the bottom.
4. Cook for 1-2 minutes & flip with large spatula to cook the other side for 1-2 minutes.
5. Stack crepes on a plate and serve with fillings on the side.

Favorite Filling Combinations

- Strawberries, Nutella, whipped cream
- Chocolate, Bananas, whipped cream
- Caramel, Bananas, chocolate chips
- Turkey, pesto, cheese, tomatoes
- Taco meat, cheese, salsa
- Eggs, bacon, cheese
- Turkey, mashed potatoes, cranberry sauce
- Ham, cheese, raspberry sauce
- Chicken, broccoli, cheese

December 17

Now having been questioned by the Pharisees as to when the kingdom of God was coming, He answered them and said, "The kingdom of God is not coming with signs to be observed; nor will they say, 'Look, here it is!' or, 'There it is!' For behold, the kingdom of God is in your midst." Luke 17:20-21

Devotional

First century Jewish culture was boxed in on all sides by the Roman government, after hundreds of years of oppression by other foreign lands. The Jews had become a culture of "someday our Savior will come," as foretold in Scripture. Their idea of the Kingdom of God coming in their lifetime was a hopeful expectation with many interpretations.

Would the Savior be a mighty military leader? Would He overthrow the oppressive government and lead them out, just as Moses led them out of Egypt? Jesus offered a plain statement by asking them to simply observe: Behold, the kingdom of God is in your midst. It's here! It's now! One way to see God's kingdom is to see the people all around, who have immediate needs that can be met.

Parents, one of the greatest areas of ministry is your home. There is no need to wait for a position at work or even in the church to begin doing meaningful ministry to impact the next generation. Simply sitting and reading with them, doing an activity together, or just listening to them talk about what is important to them is part of an emotional bonding experience that they will never forget.

It's a misleading notion that the more we do, the more

significant our efforts become. There is so much to accomplish in the daily support and love of your children. The kingdom of God is in your midst today until we live in His eternal kingdom forever in heaven. Make the most of your time on earth with the people He has given you.

Prayer

Lord, help me not to miss the precious people in front of me! Show me how to turn my attention to them when they need me, and how to invest in their emotional and spiritual health. Remind me how much they need my love and attention. Amen.

December 18

But Jesus called for them, saying, "Permit the children to come to Me, and do not hinder them, for the kingdom of God belongs to such as these. Truly I say to you, whoever does not receive the kingdom of God like a child will not enter it at all." Luke 18:16-17

Devotional

One of the sweetest and most sobering passages of scripture is when Jesus invited the children into His presence. He displayed a value for the "least of these," which in that time period, included women and children. Not only do we see a display of love and consideration for young people, but an acceptance of those who can do very little in return.

In a society dependent on labor, children were not useful to the working class until they reached a certain age. They were fully dependent on their families and were expected to obey without question according to the order of healthy family life. Children trusted that their parents would provide what was needed.

Jesus used this youthful and innocent trust as an example of how we should respond to entering the kingdom; not assuming that we've earned it, but with open and empty hands. When your kids run to you for safety, do you expect them to bring you a gift, or a list of all the good things they've done that day? Would you love them any more if they did?

In the same way, Jesus says that coming to God like a sweet child, full of trust and hope, is all we need to be accepted and be a part of the family.

There is nothing more we need to do to earn that love, and nothing we need to show to prove we're worthy.

Prayer

Lord, thank You for loving me just as I am! I have trouble believing this as an adult because I'm so used to proving my worth. Help me to rest easily in Your love and believe I am accepted, forgiven, and clean because of Jesus' sacrifice for me. Thank You, again, for sending Your Son to this earth. Amen.

O Holy Night

O holy night!
The stars are brightly shining
It is the night of the dear Savior's birth!
Long lay the world in sin and error pining
Till he appear'd and the soul felt its worth.
A thrill of hope the weary soul rejoices
For yonder breaks a new and glorious morn!

Fall on your knees
Oh hear the angel voices
Oh night divine
Oh night when Christ was born
Oh night divine
Oh night divine

Led by the light of Faith serenely beaming
With glowing hearts by His cradle we stand
So led by light of a star sweetly gleaming
Here come the wise men from Orient land
The King of Kings lay thus in lowly manger
In all our trials born to be our friend

Truly He taught us to love one another
His law is love and His gospel is peace
Chains shall He break for the slave is our brother
And in His name all oppression shall cease
Sweet hymns of joy in grateful chorus raise we,
Let all within us praise His holy name

Matthew 1-2   1 Timothy 6:15

Luke 2:1-20   Revelation 19:16

John 13:34-35

Manger Snack Mix

- Pretzel Sticks
- Crispix Cereal
- Teddy Grahams (or your favorite animal crackers)
- Mini Marshmallows
- Coco Puffs
- Cinnamon Toast Crunch
- Popcorn
- Red & Green M&Ms

Combine all ingredients together in whatever amount you prefer. Serve in cups, gift bags for neighbors and friends, or paper cones for holiday gatherings.

December 19

As He was going, they were spreading their coats on the road. As soon as He was approaching, near the descent of the Mount of Olives, the whole crowd of the disciples began to praise God joyfully with a loud voice for all the miracles which they had seen, shouting: "Blessed is the King who comes in the name of the Lord; Peace in heaven and glory in the highest!" Luke 19:36-38

Devotional

The day had come: the Triumphal Entry, one of the few accounts of Jesus listed in all four Gospels (Matthew 21, Mark 11, Luke 19, & John 12). Jesus' influence had grown, and even though He knew the end was near in Jerusalem, the very act of riding in on a donkey was another Old Testament prophecy fulfilled (Zechariah 9:9).

This act of praise and loyalty from the people was not because they recognized this fulfillment, but communicated loyalty to him as a leader, hoping this was the beginning of the overthrow of Rome. They were short-sighted, but little did they know that every event leading up to His trial and death was to prove the greatest authority of His divinity.

We can praise God and thank Him for the miracles we witness, but do we remember to praise Him in difficult times? It's plain to see Him riding in victoriously, at church or around other Christians in a nice worship service, but His promises are just as relevant and real as we're facing doubt and hopelessness.

While there is a beautiful place for worship and reverence, we can also praise Him in the dark of night, when we're alone, and needing that close friend to whisper, "Everything is going to be alright." He is good and He is God — the suffering servant who entered the world with no pretenses and left His Spirit to continue to guide us.

Prayer

Lord, I can't begin to fathom Your plan to save us, which began when You were a small and helpless baby. You have been our mighty conqueror from the beginning. Thank You for being here with me through the good and the bad. Amen.

December 20

But Jesus looked at them and said, "What then is this that is written: 'The stone which the builders rejected, This became the chief corner stone?'"
Luke 20:17

Devotional

Jesus references King David's Psalm 118:22 passage here, directly comparing Himself to David as the rejected stone. Great buildings like the temple needed strong stones to form their foundation. When a quarry stone cutter considered a stone unfit for the structure, it would be tossed aside for a better option that fit the plan of the builder.

Just as David was rejected by Saul, and overcome with grief at the pursuit of his enemies, Jesus made the direct connection from this well-known Jewish teaching that the Messiah would be rejected. Then He continued the analogy and placed Himself as the most important piece of the building: the cornerstone, which held the entire structure together. The Pharisees immediately understood His blasphemous meaning, and were ready to arrest Him were it not for the loyalty of his followers.

The Jewish leaders carried many expectations about how their Messiah would come and Jesus, once again, turned these assumptions upside down using their own traditions to prove He was the new way to God. His story was always part of the plan, but the religious leaders were too stuck in tradition to recognize what the Scriptures revealed all along. You may be faced with expectations to carry on old traditions this holiday season. Maybe you want to start something new, or make decisions outside of the influence of family.

Sometimes we're afraid to break the mold of "the way it's always been" because others may not understand your need for something new. Be encouraged that it's okay to make a change if your family needs a break. There is no need to explain yourself to make others feel better. Stand up for the change that needs to happen, and rejoin the group later when you've been refreshed and renewed.

Prayer

Lord, thank You for breaking the mold of old traditions, and for making the way of salvation for all of us. Help me to break free from practices that no longer hold meaning and guide me to start new things. Amen.

O Little Town of Bethlehem

O little town of Bethlehem, how still we see thee lie!
Above thy deep and dreamless sleep, the silent stars go by.
Yet in thy dark streets shineth, the everlasting Light;
The hopes and fears of all the years are met in thee tonight.

O morning stars, together, proclaim the holy birth!
And praises sing to God the King, and peace to men on earth.
For Christ is born of Mary, and gathered all above,
While mortals sleep the angels keep
Their watch of wondering love.

How silently, how silently the wondrous gift is given;
So God imparts to human hearts the blessings of His Heaven.
No ear may hear His coming, but in this world of sin,
Where meek souls will receive Him still,
The dear Christ enters in.

Where children pure and happy pray to the blessed Child,
Where misery cries out to Thee, Son of the Mother mild;
Where Charity stands watching and Faith holds wide the door,
The dark night wakes, the glory breaks,
And Christmas comes once more

O holy Child of Bethlehem, descend to us, we pray!
Cast out our sin and enter in, be born in us to-day.
We hear the Christmas angels, the great glad tidings tell;
O come to us, abide with us, Our Lord Emmanuel!

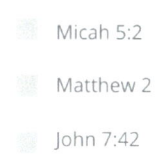

Micah 5:2

Matthew 2

John 7:42

Resurrection Rolls

- 1 package refrigerated Crescent Rolls
- 1 bag large marshmallows
- 1/2 cup melted butter
- 1/2 cup white sugar
- 2 Tbsp cinnamon

1. Preheat oven to 350°
2. Grease a muffin tin pan (or use cupcake paper liners to save on mess) and set aside.
3. Melt butter in a small bowl & mix together cinnamon & sugar in a separate shallow dish.
4. Unroll the crescent dough and separate the triangles (see dough perforations).
5. Roll the marshmallow in butter and then in the cinnamon and sugar mixture.
6. Place the marshmallow onto a dough triangle near the bigger end. Wrap each side of the dough up and over the marshmallow. Make sure every side of the dough is pinched sealed over the marshmallow.
7. Dip the rolled dough in butter and roll in the cinnamon/sugar mix before placing in the greased muffin tin. Repeat until all of the dough has been used.
8. Bake for 15 minutes.
9. Allow to cool then have kids open the "tomb" (rolls), or cut through the roll and show the kids how the "tomb" is now empty.

Dough = the tomb where Jesus was laid after his crucifixion
Marshmallow = Jesus
Butter, Cinnamon, Sugar = oils and spices that was rubbed on Jesus after his death before they placed him in the tomb.
Dough = the tomb where they buried Jesus.

Before cutting, ask if the kids remember what happened on the third day, or why we celebrate Easter. Remind them that when they went to the tomb where Jesus was buried, the tomb was empty because Jesus rose from the dead.

December 21

And while some were talking about the temple, that it was adorned with beautiful stones and votive gifts, He said, "As for these things which you are looking at, the days will come in which there will not be left one stone upon another which will not be torn down. Luke 21:5-6

Devotional

During His time in Jerusalem, Jesus walked with His disciples through the magnificent temple, at that time, under construction at the order of King Herod. A temple first built by King Solomon and destroyed by the Babylonians, this majestic symbol of Jewish tradition shone brightly in Jerusalem. We can imagine how exquisitely the decor shone from the walls and ceilings to represent the splendor of this iconic structure.

The temple, no doubt, served as a symbol to the Jewish people to represent the hardship they had endured over hundreds of years of captivity at the hands of foreign kings. But as Jesus walked through with His disciples, immediately after noticing a widow who gave everything she had to the treasury (only He could have known that), made this unnerving statement: *not one stone left upon another.*

What? This beautiful building that represented security and safety from the Roman world would be destroyed? Again?

Not a very comforting thought.

Notice the context of the last two chapters. Jesus' teaching had focused on purifying one's heart and not being like the Pharisees who flaunted their riches, wore fine clothes and asked for preferential treatment. Little did they realize, all of that false security would crumble, literally and figuratively.

If our security is grounded in where we live, the size of our bank account, or what we look like, Jesus assures us that none of these will last. Will you trust Him when the outside image is no more? Will He still be good? Just as a loving Father would, He gives us the truth so that we are not surprised when the temporary fades.

Prayer

Lord, help me to see the things that I've been valuing above the very simple need for You. Remind me of Your ever-present provision and security when I trust You. Amen.

December 22

And when He had taken some bread and given thanks, He broke it and gave it to them, saying, "This is My body which is given for you; do this in remembrance of Me." And in the same way He took the cup after they had eaten, saying, "This cup which is poured out for you is the new covenant in My blood. Luke 22:19-20

And He withdrew from them about a stone's throw, and He knelt down and began to pray, saying, "Father, if You are willing, remove this cup from Me; yet not My will, but Yours be done." Luke 22:41-42

Devotional

In the last days of Jesus' life on earth, we see a tremendous amount of stress on His human body. He knew what would happen to Him. He prepared his disciples for this time, even when they could not fully grasp the sequence of events. He established the last communion supper for them and for us to remember what He would walk through for us.

Obedience is a difficult thing to grasp when the reason is not plainly laid out. You may have gone rounds with your kids about why they need to trust that you know better. Not everything is easily explained without the bigger picture that often comes with more life experience and context.

When we see the tortured mental state of our Lord's experience from the table to the garden, we can appreciate His struggle, even with the full knowledge of events, wrestled with the reality of His humanity and His love for us. This road of His obedience was rough, even when He knew the reason.

Has God been calling you into obedience today? Have you been avoiding His leading? Take comfort in knowing that He, too, was faced with awful choices, and you, too can overcome them. "I know it's hard," He says. "But it's better on the other side."

Prayer

Lord, help me to trust You and obey when I cannot fully understand what You're doing. Thank You for holding me and walking with me and reminding me that I'm not alone in this struggle. Amen.

Silent Night

Silent night, holy night!
All is calm, all is bright.
Round yon Virgin, Mother and Child.
Holy infant so tender and mild,
Sleep in heavenly peace,
Sleep in heavenly peace.

Silent night, holy night!
Shepherds quake at the sight.
Glories stream from heaven afar
Heavenly hosts sing Alleluia,
Christ the Savior is born!
Christ the Savior is born.

Silent night, holy night!
Son of God love's pure light.
Radiant beams from Thy holy face
With dawn of redeeming grace,
Jesus Lord, at Thy birth.
Jesus Lord, at Thy birth.

Matthew 1, 2

Luke 2:8-20

Yummy Pumpkin Soup

- 3 cups chicken broth
- 1/2 tsp salt
- 2 cups pumpkin puree (canned or from scratch if you prefer)
- 1/2 cup diced onion
- 1/4 tsp dried thyme (or 1/2 tsp chopped fresh)
- 1 clove minced garlic
- 1/8 ground pepper
- 1/8 tsp ground ginger (1/2 tsp freshly grated)
- 1/4 tsp ground cinnamon
- 1/8 tsp ground nutmeg
- 1/2 cup heavy whipping cream (or coconut milk)

Garnish with...
4-5 pieces cooked bacon chopped (optional)
Freshly grated Parmesan (optional)
Sour cream or plain Greek yogurt (optional)

1. Combine all ingredients except cream / milk. Bring to a boil. Reduce heat to low & simmer for 30 minutes, uncovered.
2. With a food processor or blender, purée soup in small batches (1 cup at a time). Or, use a hand held immersion blender to blend directly in the pot. Return soup to pot and bring to a boil.
3. Reduce heat to low and simmer for another 30 minutes, uncovered. Remove from heat and stir in cream or coconut milk.
4. Pour into serving bowls. If desired, top with chopped cooked bacon, parmesan and/or sour cream / yogurt.

December 23

And Jesus, crying out with a loud voice, said, "Father, into Your hands I commit My spirit." Having said this, He breathed His last. Now when the centurion saw what had happened, he began praising God, saying, "Certainly this man was innocent." Luke 23:46-47

Devotional

We witness here the reason Jesus was born. We began when this baby entered the world and angels rejoiced because they knew this moment would come. Here, we witness the end of His suffering, even as the last breath escaped his lungs. This young Jewish radical, given an unjust trial, beaten to a pulp, and nailed to a cross in front of God and everyone, only to die a criminal's death.

The comment from this Roman centurion was not just a cruel irony, but a personal testimony from one who had witnessed countless crucifixions. This one was different. This man did not deserve what He received.

Not everyone will appreciate the difficult road you have walked until that road is over. Your kids may never say "thank you" until they become a parent themselves. Your spouse may not verbalize their love as often as you need to hear it. Your innermost heart and best intentions are between you and God, and if you remember through the pages of this devotional, He knows what you need.

Many will see, hear, and feel the impact you've made on their lives. Fewer will be prompted to say it out loud. Until that day comes, we cannot depend on others to tell us who we are, or fear being taken advantage of or stop moving forward when the feedback isn't there. Jesus knew who He was, what He needed to do, and did not allow others to define Him.

We can be 100% certain of God's love for us today because we've just witnessed the lengths that Jesus went through for us before we even existed.

Prayer

Lord, You did this for me... because I'm that valuable to You. Help me to remember Your love and acceptance every day. I have been seen, heard, and loved by You all this time. Amen.

December 24

Now He said to them, "These are My words which I spoke to you while I was still with you, that all things which are written about Me in the Law of Moses and the Prophets and the Psalms must be fulfilled." Then He opened their minds to understand the Scriptures, and He said to them, "Thus it is written, that the Christ would suffer and rise again from the dead the third day, and that repentance for forgiveness of sins would be proclaimed in His name to all the nations, beginning from Jerusalem." Luke 24:44-47

Devotional

This baby from the manger, this carpenter of Nazareth, this Rabbi of the people — fulfilled His purpose on earth: to live as Emmanuel (God with us) as promised in the Law of Moses, the word of the prophets, and the Psalms of King David. All of these prophecies set hundreds of years before Jesus' earthly birth prove that this man transcended space and time to bring the love of God to us: a people who ultimately rejected Him.

But here He sits. In a resurrected body, nothing left to do but to display the miracle of His return, and He chooses to teach them again.

Even the most patient teachers need to call up the courage to repeat themselves over and over again. If you've ever taught a child who needs to see and hear and practice multiple times before they get it, you know what I mean. The only thing that keeps a teacher or parent that engaged in the child's learning is a strong desire for their success.

Love held Him on the cross, and love led Him to the beaches to find His followers and remind them one more time that this experience was not in vain. He helped to solidify their life's purpose and mission out of tremendous love for them, and for you and I.

Prayer

Lord, You are amazing! You've shown me time and time again how extravagant Your love is for Your people. You point us back to Your Word to remind us that You made a way when there was no way. Thank You for being the way, the truth, and the path to eternal life with You. Amen.

The First Noel

The First Noel, the Angels did say
Was to certain poor shepherds in fields as they lay
In fields where they lay keeping their sheep
On a cold winter's night that was so deep.

Noel, Noel, Noel, Noel
Born is the King of Israel!

They looked up and saw a star
Shining in the East beyond them far
And to the earth it gave great light
And so it continued both day and night.

And by the light of that same star
Three Wise men came from country far
To seek for a King was their intent
And to follow the star wherever it went.

This star drew nigh to the northwest
O'er Bethlehem it took its rest
And there it did both Pause and stay
Right o'er the place where Jesus lay.

Then entered in those Wise men three
Full reverently upon their knee
And offered there in His presence
Their gold and myrrh and frankincense.

Then let us all with one accord
Sing praises to our heavenly Lord
That hath made Heaven and earth of nought
And with his blood mankind has bought.

Matthew 2:1-12   Galatians 3:13-15

Luke 2:10-13   Ephesians 1:17

Cranberry Pudding Cake
with Orange Butter Sauce

Our family's Christmas Eve tradition with a little twist of orange

CAKE

- 1 cup sugar
- 3 tablespoons salted butter (softened)
- 1 cup whole milk
- 1/2 tsp vanilla
- 2 cups all-purpose flour
- 2 tsp baking powder
- 1/2 teaspoon salt
- 2 cups fresh cranberries (chopped)

BUTTER SAUCE

- 2/3 cup orange juice
- 1 Tbsp unsalted butter
- 1/2 cup sugar
- 1/2 tsp cornstarch

CAKE

1. Preheat the oven to 350º. Grease an 8×8 baking pan with cooking spray or butter.
2. In a large bowl, use a whisk or electric mixer to mix together the sugar and butter.
3. Add the milk and vanilla extract. Mix again.
4. Stir in flour, baking powder & salt. Mix on slow speed until barely combined (on low speed). Do not over-mix.
5. Fold in chopped cranberries.
6. Pour and spread the batter in the greased pan.
7. Bake for 40 minutes. The cake should test done in the center when poked with a toothpick or bounce back when you touch it.

BUTTER SAUCE

1. Set aside 1 tsp of orange juice in a small bowl.
2. In a small saucepan on medium heat, melt butter.
3. Whisk in remaining orange juice, & sugar.
4. Bring mixture to a low boil and cook for 10 minutes to reduce the liquid.
5. Whisk the cornstarch into the previously set aside orange juice until smooth, then add to mixture. Continue to whisk for about one minute.
6. Remove from heat and let cool to thicken. Serve warm over cake.

December 25

You are witnesses of these things. And behold, I am sending forth the promise of My Father upon you; but you are to stay in the city until you are clothed with power from on high. Luke 24:48-49

Devotional

In 25 days, you have walked through the birth and ministry of Jesus. You have read the testimonies of angels, shepherds, blind, lame, and broken people: all changed forever because of God's promises fulfilled.

This is one of the last recorded statements Jesus made to His disciples, just before the famous "go into all the world" scripture. That was their direction, but not before He promised to prepare them one last time. "The promise of My Father," and "power on high" was to come in God's third form, the Holy Spirit.

The same Spirit of God dwelling in us when we choose to follow, listen and obey. God made a way to clothe us in His Spirit — to have Him near us in all circumstances, to guide and tutor us through this life. Do you believe He is with you even now? He knows what you're going through — from the joy to the pain. You were made to be a witness to the work He has done and will continue to do in your life.

Reach out to Him this Christmas. He's always there. If you've felt distant from Him lately, invite Him to be the Lord of your every day. Even if You've known Him for years, renew your relationship today, admit that You need Him, and fall into His open arms.

Prayer

Lord Jesus, what an awesome life You led on earth. I recognize that Your love for me led You from the manger of Bethlehem all the way to the cross of Calvary. Thank You for forgiving me, even before I was born, knowing that I would be a sinner in need of a Savior. Help me to lead my family through Your Word and in Your grace and truth. In Jesus' name. Amen.

Afterward

This Christmas may have been different from Christmases you have celebrated in the past. The aftermath of pandemic isolation, and relationships with family may look different now.

Even after you have gone through this devotion, you may be putting away decorations and thinking, "What now? Will the wonder of awe of Christmas go away until next year?"

The good news is, it doesn't have to, because the real good news is the gospel. God loved us so much, that He came down as a baby, lived among us as a man, and sacrificed His life on a cross so we could be reconciled to Him forever (John 3:16).

After spending twenty-five days with Jesus, being a witness to His life, and participating in Luke's gospel account, I hope you sensed the presence of Jesus as God on earth. Living. Breathing. Healing. Active.

Jesus is as real as you and I, and He wants you to trust the presence of His Spirit in your life even now. Right this minute.

Will you trust Him with your life today?

Just talk to Him. It's okay, He hears you.

Talk to Him about the stress and tension you've been feeling lately.

Talk to Him about how you can't figure out the next part of your life.

Talk to Him about the burden of decisions that have been weighing on your heart.

God doesn't expect you to have all the answers, or do all the good things to earn His love. You are loved simply as you are. But He knew you couldn't live this life without Him.

That's why He came.

Whatever stage of life you're in right now, I promise you that He understands and wants you to be free.

Pray - God, I don't always know what to do, but I want to believe You're always with me. Help me when I don't believe. Help me when I'm scared and I don't know who to talk to. Help me when I don't think I need help. I want to start this new year well, and to sense Your presence in my life. Help me to trust You even when I can't see what's coming. Thank you for always knowing the way. Please show me Your goodness in every circumstance. Please forgive me for my sinful heart and make me clean. I want to be sensitive to Your leading and a loving example to my family. In Jesus' name, amen.

Special Thanks

To my Lord and Savior Jesus Christ - I met you as a baby in church and have fallen in love with your Word and been led by Your gentle Spirit as an adult. You've been walking with me through every storm and rough season. Thank you for Your sacrifice on the cross and the precious gift of salvation.

Thank you to my husband Bruce, who's support is invaluable. Your passion for Biblical truth inspires our family to dig deeper, ask questions, and stay connected to God's Word.

My almost teenagers - Chloe and Asher, you are fun and silly, and such curious learners. Thank you for working with me as we figure out homeschool every day, and for giving me the time and space to write. You will do amazing things with your own talents and gifts. Keep being curious.

To my parents, Scott and Valerie. You built such a strong foundation of Jesus in our lives and kept Him at the forefront of our childhood. I am forever grateful for your faithfulness to His Word, and your examples of love and grace in my life. Thank you for encouraging me in this journey, and for opening your home for Christmas each year to carry on these beautiful traditions.

To my sister Jaclyn, who is usually the first person I call in the morning. You make me better every day by talking me up when I need a lift, and talking me down from the ledge when I want to quit. Thank you for sharing in my love for all things Christmas and carrying on favorite traditions to all of our kids.

My brothers Josh and Jonah - I love being with you and your beautiful families at Christmas time. Thank you for always making me laugh and think about meaningful topics. I love watching you both grow into strong and confident men of God.

Pastor Waxer and Cindy Tipton, and the staff of One Love Ministries: Thank you for faithfully teaching God's Word, and equipping the saints throughout the Hawaiian islands. Your influence on the church is making our community stronger, and a more compassionate presence.

To my sister from another mister - Dawn. You've been there on my lowest days and celebrated my wins when I didn't believe I was valuable. Thank you for seeing me through the emotional turmoil of my relationships, and for pointing me back to Jesus.

Kanani, my sweet friend and writer extraordinaire. Thank you for clearing the blurry path for me to become a better writer. Your insight and encouragement is invaluable, and I look forward to the words you continue to put out into the world.

To my sister in ministry - Karen, your gentle approach to loving others well is so comforting. Thank you for your honesty, your warmth, and compassion to see women healed and whole. Your love for Jesus, His Word, and time in prayer in inspiring.

To my right hand, and seriously funny hānai sister - Jordan, your help and support has been invaluable to me these past few years. But more than that, you are just an amazing person. I can't wait to see what God has for your future.

To Roger Kathi Lipp and all the amazing writers who have been mentored through your ministry. I am forever grateful for my time at the Red House and for the gentle nudges you've given me to press forward in writing. Thank you for helping me to find confidence in myself and God's purpose for my life.

Listen to the

Audio Book

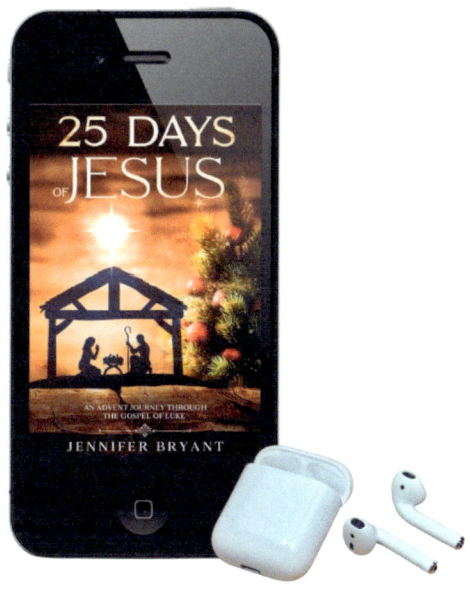

Scan the code below for 10% off

Christmas Songs
PLAYLIST

Scan the code below to access the playlist and sing along with the lyrics.

Thank You Postcards

Scan the code below to order your Thank You postcards. Teaching our kids gratitude one written note at a time.

Christmas Recipes

Spinach & Bacon ⬭
with Sweet Potato C⬭

- 2 Sweet Potatoes (medium, or
  peeled, sliced 1/8" or 4 cups s⬭
- 3 slices bacon, diced
- 2 garlic cloves
- 1 yellow onion, diced
- 8 large eggs
- 3/4 cup milk (can use almond⬭
- 1/8 tsp ground nutmeg
- 1 handful grated cheese (che⬭
- 16 oz. chopped spinach (fro⬭
  2 cups fresh)
- 4 Tbsp coconut oil (separate⬭

1. Preheat oven to 360°
2. Grease bottom and sides ⬭
   dish with coconut oil
3. Peel and slice sweet potat⬭
   circles on dish to cover bo⬭
4. Bake at 360° for 15 minut⬭
5. While crust is baking, wa⬭
   oil in frying pan.
6. Sautee garlic & onion un⬭
7. Stir often to prevent burn⬭
   cook down until crust is r⬭
8. Remove cooked mixture ⬭
   & cook until sizzling. Add⬭
   & spread over sweet pot⬭
9. Scramble eggs with mil⬭
   nutmeg. Pour into crust,⬭
10. Bake for 25-30 minutes⬭

Make Ahead
French Toast Casserole

- 1 package brioche bread
- 8 eggs, large
- 2 cups milk
- 1/4 cup maple syrup
- 1 Tbsp vanilla extract
- 1/2 tsp salt
- 1 tsp cinnamon
- 1/4 tsp nutmeg
- 2 Tbsp coconut oil
- 1 cup pecans, chopped (optional)

Topping
- 1/2 cup light brown sugar
- 1 tsp cinnamon
- 4 Tbsp salted butter, sliced cold

Prepare and Chill Overnight
1. Grease 9'x13' baking dish with coconut oil
2. Cut bread into 1' cubes and layer in dish with
   chopped pecans
3. Whisk together eggs, milk, syrup, vanilla, salt,
   cinnamon, & nutmeg
4. Pour over bread & pecans
5. Cover with foil and chill for 4-6 hours

Ready to Bake
1. Remove casserole from refrigerator & preheat
   oven to 350°
2. Mix brown sugar, cinnamon, & sliced butter
   together. Crumble over casserole
3. Cover dish with foil & bake at 350° for 30
   minutes.
4. Uncover & bake for another 20 minutes.
5. Let cool, then slice & serve with powdered sugar
   & maple syrup. Serves 8-10.

⬭nberry Pinwheels

- ⬭tortillas
- ⬭e, softened
- ⬭berries
- ⬭⬭
- ⬭e slices
- ⬭aves, without ribs

- ⬭ cheese, & cranberries
- ⬭de by side, overlap slightly
- ⬭r both tortillas
- ⬭s, & lettuce
- ⬭ard and roll tightly like a

- ⬭ap in plastic wrap & store in

- ⬭into 1' pieces. Leftovers
- ⬭erves 2-4.

Scan the code below to download the
full recipe book

Scan the code below to subscribe on
iTunes or wherever you listen to podcasts!

About the Author

Jennifer Bryant is a writer and podcaster at PracticalFamily.org. She interviews influencers all over North America to encourage mothers to live out their calling in strength and grace. She is the host of the Practical Family Podcast and coaches moms through their homeschooling journey.

Jennifer holds a degree in Christian Studies (Bible Theology and Philosophy), certification in Christian apologetics and Master's level training in education. She hosts book studies with women and families in person and online on motherhood, parenting, and Biblical education.

She and her husband Bruce have been married 15 years and together they own (he operates) the best fish taco shop in town. They live just outside of Waikiki in Honolulu, Hawaii and are raising two precious pre-teens and enjoying homeschooling in Hawaii and on the road as often as they can travel.

Follow her fun videos of family and mom life on Facebook, Instagram, and TikTok. Podcast interviews available on YouTube.

Family Memories

_____

_____

_____

_____

_____

_____

_____

_____

_____

_____

_____

_____

_____

_____

_____

_____

_____

_____

Family Memories

_____

_____

_____

_____

_____

_____

_____

_____

_____

_____

_____

_____

_____

_____

_____

_____

_____

_____

Family Memories

_____

_____

_____

_____

_____

_____

_____

_____

_____

_____

_____

_____

_____

_____

_____

_____

_____

Family Memories

_____

_____

_____

_____

_____

_____

_____

_____

_____

_____

_____

_____

_____

_____

_____

_____

_____

_____

Family Memories

_____

_____

_____

_____

_____

_____

_____

_____

_____

_____

_____

_____

_____

_____

_____

_____

_____

Made in the USA
Columbia, SC
05 December 2024

6295def3-be08-4f3a-8937-2a42a1a66e7bR01